preteen Bible study series

The Bible and Me

Group

Loveland, Colorado

Group's R.E.A.L. Guarantee to you:

This Group resource incorporates our R.E.A.L. approach to ministry—one that encourages long-term retention and life transformation. It's ministry that's:

Relational
Because learner-to-learner interaction enhances learning and builds Christian friendships.

Experiential
Because what learners experience through discussion and action sticks with them up to 9 times longer than what they simply hear or read.

Applicable
Because the aim of Christian education is to equip learners to be both hearers and doers of God's Word.

Learner-based
Because learners understand and retain more when the learning process takes into consideration how they learn best.

preteen Bible study series

The Bible and Me

Visit our Web site: **www.grouppublishing.com**

Credits
Author: Paul Woods
Editor: Jim Hawley
Creative Development Editor: Karl Leuthauser
Chief Creative Officer: Joani Schultz
Copy Editor: Deirdre Brouer
Art Director: Kari K. Monson
Cover Art Director/Designer: Jeff A. Storm
Cover Photographer: Daniel Treat
Print Production Artist: Tracy K. Hindman
Illustrator: Shawn Banner
Production Manager: DeAnne Lear

ISBN 0-7644-2480-7
10 9 8 7 6 5 4 3 2 1   12 11 10 09 08 07 06 05 04 03

Printed in the United States of America.

Contents

Introduction:
The Bible and Me

The Bible can be an intimidating book for preteens. Many preteens may have grown up listening to Bible stories or focused on memorizing Bible verses. But now preteens are at a point in their development where they can dig deeper into the truths of Scripture, and this study will help them do just that!

The Bible and Me will help preteens both understand the Bible and apply it to their lives. The first study focuses on how God guided the formation of the Scriptures to create the commonly accepted thirty-nine Old Testament books and twenty-seven New Testament books that make up most Bibles.

> Preteens are at a point in their development where they can dig deeper into the truths of Scripture.

Next your students will explore how the Bible can be a handbook for life. Preteens will discover how God's Word can guide them in their daily lives.

In the third study, preteens will discover a variety of Bible learning tools. They will practice using these tools to provide biblical answers to whatever questions they may ask.

The last study will explore how preteens can set up a personal Bible study plan. Preteens will examine different methods of study and make commitments to spend time with God in his message of hope for us all!

About Faith 4 Life: Preteen Bible Study Series

The Faith 4 Life: Preteen Bible Study Series helps preteens take a Bible-based approach to faith and life issues. Each book in the series contains these important elements:

- **Life application of Bible truth**—Faith 4 Life studies help preteens understand what the Bible says and then apply that truth to their lives.

- **A relevant topic**—Each Faith 4 Life book focuses on one main topic, with four studies to give your students a thorough understanding of how the Bible relates to that topic.

- **One point**—Each study makes one point, centering on that one theme to make sure students really understand the important truth it conveys. This point is stated upfront and throughout the study.

- **Simplicity**—The studies are easy to use. Each contains a "Before the Study" box that outlines any advance preparation required. Each study also contains a "Study at a Glance" chart so you can quickly and easily see what supplies you'll need and what each study will involve.

- **Action and interaction**—Each study relies on experiential learning to help students learn what God's Word has to say. Preteens discuss and debrief their experiences in large groups, small groups, and individual reflection.

- **Reproducible handouts**—Faith 4 Life books include reproducible handouts for students so that there is no need for student books.

- **Flexible options**—Faith 4 Life preteen studies have two opening and two closing activities. Choose the options that work best for your students, time frame, or supply needs.

- **Follow-up ideas**—At the end of each book, you'll find a section called "Changed 4 Life." This section provides ideas for following up with your students to make sure the Bible truths stick with them.

Use Faith 4 Life studies to show your preteens how the Bible is relevant to their lives. Help them see that God can invade every area of their lives and change them in ways they can only imagine. Encourage your students to go deeper into faith—faith that will sustain them for life! Faith 4 Life, forever!

The Timeless Word

The Point: ➤God guided the formation of the Scriptures to bring his hopeful message to us.

Preteens may see the Bible as an old book that has little relevance to their lives. But though the Bible is old, it reveals God's timeless message to us. God used a number of authors who used a variety of literary styles throughout hundreds of years to compose his message.

Use this study to help preteens see God's message of hope and salvation to all who cling to the truth of his everlasting Word!

Scripture Source

Deuteronomy 31:9-13

Moses gave instructions on how God's law should be passed down to Jews and non-Jews throughout the generations so that they would learn to fear the Lord.

Mark 12:28-34

Jesus explains to one of the teachers of the law that the most important commandment is to love God with all your heart, soul, mind, and strength (Deuteronomy 6:4-5). This summarizes the first four of the Ten Commandments. Then Jesus says to love your neighbor as yourself, which summarizes the last six commandments.

John 20:30-31

John explains that he wrote about the miracles of Jesus so that people would believe in Jesus as God's Son.

2 Timothy 3:15-16

Paul instructs Timothy that the Scriptures point to salvation through faith in Jesus and guide us to live godly lives.

The Study at a Glance

Section	Minutes	What Students Will Do	Supplies
Warm-Up Option 1	up to 10	**Silent Message**—Convey a message to their partners without talking.	Pens, paper, "Message Instructions" box (p. 8)
Warm-Up Option 2	up to 10	**Making Sure**—Recite the definition of the word *sure* from memory.	Dictionary, newsprint, marker
Bible Connection	up to 15	**How the Word Was Chosen**—Choose which statements from a list are found in the Bible, then hear how the New Testament was formed.	Pens, "And God Said…or Didn't" handouts (p. 13)
	up to 15	**The Bible's Purpose**—Explore Deuteronomy 31:9-13; John 20:30-31; and 2 Timothy 3:15-16, then create presentations that show why God gave us the Bible.	Bibles, newsprint, markers, treats
Life Application	up to 15	**Word Wisdom**—Explore Mark 12:28-34, and list ways to use the Bible in everyday life.	Bibles, newsprint, marker, tape
Wrap-Up Option 1	up to 5	**Praise the Scriptures**—Participate in a prayer of praise to God for his Word, then commit to reading the Bible each day this week.	"Three Praises for God" handouts (p. 14), "Word for the Week 1" bookmarks (p. 12)
Wrap-Up Option 2	up to 5	**Bible Partners**—Choose partners to encourage them to read the Bible each day this week.	"Word for the Week 1" bookmarks (p. 12), index cards, pens

Before the Study

Set out Bibles, a dictionary, paper, pens, newsprint, markers, tape, treats, and index cards.

Make one photocopy of the "Message Instructions" box (p. 8) for every two preteens. Make one photocopy of the "And God Said…or Didn't" handout (p. 13) and the "Word for the Week 1" bookmark (p. 12) for each student.

If you choose to do Wrap-Up Option 1, you'll also need one photocopy of the "Three Praises for God" handout (p. 14) for each student.

The Study

Warm-Up Option 1

Silent Message *(up to 10 minutes)*

Before kids arrive, place pens and sheets of paper throughout the room. Have kids form pairs. Give one partner in each pair a photocopy of the "Message Instructions" box below, making sure the other partner can't see the instructions. Have preteens holding the "Message Instructions" box follow the instructions to communicate the message to their partners.

Give students a few minutes to communicate the message.

Ask: • **How did you communicate your message without speaking?**

• **Which method of communication was most accurate? Why?**

Say: Today we're going to study an important message that's also been given to us in writing. The message comes from God communicating through human writers. ➤**God guided the formation of the Scriptures to bring his hopeful message to us. Let's explore how this happened.**

The Point ➤

Message Instructions

Communicate the message below to your partner any way you want to *without* talking.

God loves you and has big plans for your life.

Warm-Up Option 2

Making Sure *(up to 10 minutes)*

Set out a dictionary, and write the word *sure* on a sheet of newsprint. As preteens enter, have them take turns looking up the definition of *sure* in the dictionary. Caution kids not to tell each other what they find.

After at least five students—or all of them if you have time—have looked up the word, retrieve the dictionary.

Ask: • **What's the definition of *sure*? Try to tell me word-for-word.**

Allow several volunteers to give you their definitions.

Ask: • **Why do we have so many variations of the definition?**

• **What would happen to our language if there were no dictionaries?**

Say: Writing something down is the *sure* way to pass a message along to others. If a message is in writing, it doesn't change when people forget parts of it. Today we're going to study an important message that's been given to us in writing. The message comes from God communicating through human writers.

The Point ➤ ➤**God guided the formation of the Scriptures to bring his hopeful message to us. Let's explore how this happened.**

Bible Connection

How the Word Was Chosen *(up to 15 minutes)*

Form groups of three, and give each preteen an "And God Said…or Didn't" handout (p. 13). Have each group discuss the statements on the handout and decide which ones are from the Bible.

As kids discuss the statements, rotate from group to group, and give students hints to help them decide which statements are really from the Bible. The correct answers are in the "What God Said…or Didn't" box in the margin.

After groups finish their handouts, discuss which statements really are from the Bible.

Ask: • Why was it so hard to decide which statements are from the Bible?

• How did it feel not knowing which ones to choose?

• How is that similar to how the early Christians might have felt as they tried to decide what to include in the New Testament?

• How did you feel when I came around and helped you?

• How is that similar to how the early Christians might have felt, knowing the Holy Spirit was guiding them to form the Bible?

Have kids stand behind one another in single rows.

Say: I'm going to read some information about the Bible. Listen as I read, and every time I say something you already know, take a step to the right.

Read the following information aloud, pausing between sentences to allow students to move.

Say: It probably wasn't easy for the early Christians to decide which books God wanted in the New Testament. By that time, the Old Testament— the part of the Bible written before Jesus came—was already written and accepted by God's people.

But deciding what should be included in the New Testament was hard. Lots of books and letters had been written by Christians in the first one hundred years after Christ returned to heaven. And not all of them belonged in the Bible. So in the second century after Christ, the Christians decided on four basic questions to guide them in selecting which books and letters should be included in the Bible:

1. Was the book or letter written or approved by an apostle?

2. Were its contents essentially spiritual?

3. Did the book or letter show evidence of being inspired by God?

4. Had most churches accepted it?

FYI

Whenever groups discuss a list of questions, write the questions on newsprint, and tape the newsprint to the wall so that groups can discuss the questions at their own pace.

What God Said… or Didn't

1. Herman Melville
2. Rousseau
3. Ecclesiastes 7:8
4. Hugh Black
5. Thomas Carlyle
6. Proverbs 13:10
7. Proverbs 6:6
8. Pascal
9. Matthew 10:24
10. Paul Scherer
11. Song of Songs 8:7a

These questions made deciding easier. But even with God's guidance, it still took about two hundred more years to settle the issue. The Bible was finally certified as complete by a council of church leaders in 397 A.D. And it's still the same today!

After you finish reading, have kids look around at where they are.

Ask: • **Were you surprised about what you knew about how the Bible was formed? Why or why not?**

Say: **As we can see, there's a lot we don't know about how the Bible was**

The Point ➤

formed. ➤**But God guided the formation of the Scriptures to bring his hopeful message to us. Let's look at what that message is.**

FYI

If you have fewer than six preteens in your group, form one group, and assign one or two passages to the whole group. If you have time, you could assign all the passages. When you debrief each presentation, read the other passages, and ask kids to discuss any additional insights.

The Bible's Purpose *(up to 15 minutes)*

Form three groups. Assign one of these passages to each group: Deuteronomy 31:9-13; John 20:30-31; and 2 Timothy 3:15-16.

Say: **Each group has a Bible passage that helps us understand the Bible's purpose. In your group I want you to create a presentation based on your passage that shows the Bible's purpose. You have five minutes to prepare your presentation.**

Let groups choose how to create their presentations. Suggest options such as a news report, a scientific announcement, a skit, or a visual presentation, using newsprint and markers. After five minutes, have groups give their presentations.

Ask: • **What do these presentations teach you about the Bible's purpose?**

Write kids' responses on newsprint. Congratulate the kids on their responses by giving them a treat you know they'll like, such as a doughnut or candy bar. But tell them they can't eat their treats yet. Read aloud the groups' answers again.

Ask: • **So why did God give us the Bible?**

• **I gave you treats, but you haven't eaten them yet. How do you know they'll be good?**

• **How is believing that your treat is good like believing the Bible is good?**

Say: **Another way to know if something is good is to find out more information about it. The passages we presented showed the wisdom of God's**

The Point ➤

Word and how it offers hope. ➤**God guided the formation of the Scriptures to bring his hopeful message to us. But we have to choose to follow that wisdom. Let's look into this idea more.**

Let kids eat their treats as you begin the next activity.

Life Application

Word Wisdom *(up to 15 minutes)*

Say: In Jesus' day there were religious leaders and teachers. One of these teachers asked Jesus a question.

Ask a volunteer to read Mark 12:28-34 aloud to the group.

Ask: • **After Jesus answered the teacher, how did the teacher respond?**

• **What are some other ways he could have responded?**

• **How did the teacher's response show his attitude toward God's Word?**

Say: Jesus said the teacher responded wisely. And just as the teacher responded favorably to God's wisdom, we can do the same. ➤**God guided the formation of the Scriptures to bring his hopeful message to us. Let's list some ways God's wisdom from the Bible can help us.**

◀ *The Point*

Tape a piece of newsprint to the wall, and have kids brainstorm ways to use the Bible as you write down their ideas. If they have trouble getting started, give them a few suggestions, such as "God's wisdom from the Bible can help us find answers to our problems" or "God's wisdom from the Bible can guide us in making decisions about friendships."

When you've listed five or six ideas, have kids form pairs.

Say: Discuss with your partner ways you can gain more help from the wisdom in the Bible. Then choose one particular way to use the Bible this week. For example, you might say, "I'm going to look in the Bible to find out how I can have a better attitude at school."

Give kids a few minutes to discuss before the Wrap-Up.

Wrap-Up Option 1

Praise the Scriptures *(up to 5 minutes)*

Say: Let's praise God for giving us his written Word.

Give each preteen a photocopy of the "Three Praises for God" handout (p. 14). Form four groups, and have each group number off from one to four. Have groups read aloud their parts on the handout to celebrate what God has given us in his Word. Then give kids the "Word for the Week 1" bookmarks (see margin on p. 12).

Say: If we want help from the Bible, we have to read it. If you aren't already reading the Bible regularly, check out these passages this week.

Close the study with prayer, asking God to help your students use the Bible to help them this week.

Wrap-Up Option 2

Bible Partners *(up to 5 minutes)*

Give kids the "Word for the Week 1" bookmarks (see margin). Also provide index cards and pens.

Say: Here is a bookmark with daily Bible readings. God's wisdom is available to us when we take some time to read his Word. One way to help us read the Bible is through encouraging one another. Take a minute to find one or two partners, and commit to read the Bible this week. Make an agreement by exchanging phone numbers and e-mail addresses. Then each day this week, contact one another to encourage reading the Bible passages, and talk about what you are discovering from the passages.

Close the study with prayer, asking God to help your students use the Bible to help them this week.

Extra-Time Tips

In God We Trust—Form groups of three. Have each group think of a slogan that explains why we should believe God's Word. Then have groups use poster board and markers to create a poster presenting their slogans. When kids have finished, have each group present its poster, and tape the posters to the wall. Keep the posters on the wall throughout this study, then display them for the rest of the congregation to see.

Bible Jeopardy—Form two groups. Have each group think of three questions and answers about the Bible, based on today's study. Then have groups quiz each other as if they're on Jeopardy. Have the first group begin by giving one of its answers so that the other group has to provide a response in the form of a question.

And God Said...or Didn't

Some of the statements below are from the Bible. Others are from people throughout history.
Check mark the statements you think are from the Bible.

1. "He offered a prayer so deeply devout that he seemed kneeling and praying at the bottom of the sea."

2. "Do not judge, and you will never be mistaken."

3. "The end of a matter is better than its beginning, and patience is better than pride."

4. "The fear of God kills all other fears."

5. "Blessed are the valiant that have lived in the Lord."

6. "Pride only breeds quarrels, but wisdom is found in those who take advice."

7. "Go to the ant, you sluggard; consider its ways and be wise!"

8. "It is the heart which experiences God, and not the reason."

9. "A student is not above his teacher, nor a servant above his master."

10. "We find freedom when we find God; we lose it when we lose him."

11. "Many waters cannot quench love; rivers cannot wash it away."

Three Praises for God

Read aloud the following prayer to celebrate all God has given to us through his Word.

Group 1: Lord, your Word is everlasting.

Group 2: It continues forever in heaven.

All: Thanks, God, for giving us the Bible.

Group 3: Your loyalty will continue from now on.

Group 4: You made the earth, and it still stands.

All: Thanks, God, that we can trust in your Word.

Group 1: All things continue to this day because of your laws.

Group 2: All things serve you.

All: Thanks, God, for caring about us.

Group 3: We will never forget your orders,

Group 4: Because they fill us with life.

Groups 1 and 4: Thanks, God, for telling us who you are.

All: Three praises for God!

This reading is a paraphrase of Psalm 119:89-91, 93.

A Handbook for Life

The Point: ➤ God's Word shows us how to live our everyday lives.

As preteens mature, they learn new experiences and face many choices, both good and bad. They may see the Bible as an object to be respected but not as God's guide to their lives. Or they may be intimidated by its size and complexity.

But God wants the Bible to be a guide, or handbook, for life. God's Word is designed to be applied to everyday circumstances. Use this study to help preteens discover the truths that can lead them to an abundant life.

Scripture Source

Psalm 119:105-106

The psalmist uses an analogy of a lamp to describe God's Word. Just as a lamp lights one's path, God's Word gives us "light" as we are faced with the challenges of following him.

Matthew 7:24-27

Jesus concludes his Sermon on the Mount by teaching about the wise and foolish builders. Jesus compares people who follow his words to wise builders, building their homes on a rock foundation. On the other hand, those who do not follow Jesus' teachings are foolish builders whose homes are destroyed because they were built on sand.

2 Timothy 3:16-17

Paul tells Timothy the value of God's Word. He explains how Scripture is inspired by God and designed to be used for teaching and correcting in order to produce mature Christians.

The Study at a Glance

Section	Minutes	What Students Will Do	Supplies
Warm-Up Option 1	up to 10	**Our Group Handbook**—Create a handbook for new group members.	Paper, staplers, thin-tipped markers
Warm-Up Option 2	up to 10	**Handbooks for Most Anything**—Describe the purposes of different types of handbooks.	Paper, pens, a variety of handbooks or instruction manuals (see page 17)
Bible Connection	up to 15	**Following Instructions**—Contrast following or not following directions in a treasure hunt to following or not following Jesus' words in Matthew 7:24-27.	Bibles, "Treasure Instructions" handout (p. 23), snacks or treats, pen
	up to 15	**Light in the Darkness**—Experience exploring Psalm 119:105-106 with varying degrees of light, then create Bible prescriptions based on 2 Timothy 3:16-17.	Bibles, 3 flashlights or votive candles and matches, paper, pens
Life Application	up to 10	**Let God's Word Shine on Me**—Write down areas in their lives that need God's light.	Bibles, paper, pens, flashlight or votive candle and matches
Wrap-Up Option 1	up to 5	**The Word for Life**—Create slogans about how the Bible can help people.	Paper, markers, tape, "Word for the Week 2" bookmarks (p. 21)
Wrap-Up Option 2	up to 10	**The Word From the Word**—Share about their personal Bible readings from the previous week.	"Word for the Week 2" bookmarks (p. 21)

Before the Study

Set out Bibles, paper, pens, staplers, markers, snacks or treats, tape, three flashlights or three votive candles with matches, and a variety of handbooks or instruction manuals (see page 17).

Make one photocopy of the "Treasure Instructions" handout (p. 23) after following the instructions on page 18.

You'll also need one photocopy of the "Word for the Week 2" bookmark (p. 21) for each preteen.

The Study

Warm-Up Option 1

Our Group Handbook *(up to 10 minutes)*

Form groups of three or four. Give each group a sheet of paper and some thin-tipped markers. Have groups make an eight-page booklet by following these instructions: Fold the paper twice, once each way. Then staple along the crease of the last fold, and cut the other fold, creating an eight-page booklet. (See margin illustration.)

Say: Your group is going to spend a few minutes creating a new-member handbook for our entire group.

Instruct preteens to create a title page and then write down on each page what they think a new member should know about the group.

When groups have finished, ask them to share what they wrote in their handbooks.

Ask: • If you were new to our group, how would this handbook be useful to you?

• Is there anything else you might want to know that the handbooks don't tell you about our group? Explain.

Say: I asked you to quickly create a handbook to help new people feel more comfortable in our group. Although we covered some good points, I'm sure we missed some too. Today we're going to look at the Bible as a kind of handbook. But unlike our handbooks, the Bible gives us everything we need to live. Let's discover how ➤God's Word shows us how to live our everyday lives.

◀ *The Point*

Warm-Up Option 2

Handbooks for Most Anything *(up to 10 minutes)*

Before the study, collect handbooks or instruction manuals from cars, appliances, computer equipment, or other items you have at your house.

Form a group for each manual you bring to the study. Give each group a pen, sheet of paper, and one of the manuals. Have each group assign the following roles: a reader who will read some of the information in the manual, a recorder who will list some of the contents from the manual, a reporter who will share the group's research with the class, and one or more encouragers who will keep the activity on track and make sure everyone participates. If a group does not consist of enough members to fulfill each role, group members may combine roles.

Say: Each group has a handbook or instruction manual. Using the roles your group has chosen for each member, take a few minutes to research and summarize your group's handbook. After three minutes, we'll listen to each group's report.

Give groups about three minutes to prepare their reports. Have reporters share their groups' findings.

Ask: • If you owned the item described in the handbook, how would this handbook be useful to you?

• Would you use this handbook to learn more about this item? Why or why not?

Say: I asked you to quickly summarize your group's handbook. Although you covered some information in your handbooks, you also left out a lot of information. Companies provide handbooks to help you understand how to use and enjoy the item you've bought. If you chose not to read the handbook, you might not know how to properly or safely operate your item. Today we're going to look at the Bible as a kind of handbook. But unlike our handbooks, the Bible gives us something far more important than learning how to operate a computer. Let's

The Point ➤ **discover how ➤God's Word shows us how to live our everyday lives.**

Bible Connection

Following Instructions *(up to 15 minutes)*

Before the study, carefully hide a treasure, such as a bag of gold-coin candy or something else kids could share, in a place near your meeting room. Be sure it's not too easy to find. On the "Treasure Instructions" handout (p. 23), write the instructions to finding the treasure in the first box of the handout. For example, you could write, "Turn left outside our room, and walk ten steps. Turn right into the room with the blue door, then look on the shelves to your left." Don't write anything in the second box of the handout. Once you've written the instructions, make a photocopy of the handout. Then cut the photocopy of the two instruction boxes apart, and fold each one over.

Form two groups. Give each group its instructions, but tell students not to look at them yet.

Say: Each group has been given instructions to find a hidden treasure. In a minute you're going to try and find it. The group that finds the treasure gets to keep it. Your instructions are secret. Don't let the other group see your instructions.

Have groups search for the treasure.

The group with your written instructions should find the treasure quickly. The other group may quickly complain about the unfairness of the hunt. Let the complaining go on for a bit, then bring both groups together. Have the group with the treasure share it with the other group during the debriefing.

Ask: • Why was it so easy for one group to find the treasure?

• Why was it harder for the other group?

• How did the written instructions impact the group that found the treasure?

Have a volunteer read Matthew 7:24-27 aloud to the group.

Ask: • How was following the written treasure instructions like building a house on a rock?

Say: In this activity, one group couldn't follow the written instructions because there weren't any.

Ask: • How was not having any instructions to follow like building a house on the sand?

Say: Jesus tells us that following his words is like building on a firm foundation. Before you can build a building, you have to build a foundation. The Bible is like a foundation. In this activity, the group who followed the written instructions found the treasure. The other group didn't have a choice. But in real life, we all have a choice. And if we choose to follow it, ▶God's Word shows us how to live our everyday lives. Now let's look at what God says about how to use the Bible.

◀ *The Point*

FYI

If you can't find a dark room, you could drape a towel or a blanket over a table, and have your Scripture reader sit underneath the table.

Also, if you use candles, have water or a fire extinguisher nearby.

Light in the Darkness *(up to 15 minutes)*

You'll need the room to be dark or mostly dark for this activity. If this isn't possible, move to another area where it will be dark.

Light three votive candles, or give three volunteers each a flashlight. Have the volunteers stand by the candles or hold the flashlights and be prepared to blow out the candles or turn off the flashlights when you give them the signal. Keep your main lights on at this point. Ask for another volunteer to read a Scripture passage. Provide a Bible, and ask your reader to find Psalm 119:102. Turn off the main lights, and have the three volunteers light the candles or turn on the flashlights. Have your reader begin reading Psalm 119:102-106. Signal one of your volunteers to extinguish a light at this point. When the reader reads verse 103, signal the second volunteer to extinguish another light. As soon as the reader completes verse 105, signal the third volunteer to extinguish the last light. The reader may be able to finish reading, depending on how dark the room has become. When the reader is finished or stops, turn on the main lights, and discuss the following questions.

Ask: • How did the light impact the person reading?

• What happened when each light went out?

• In this passage, the psalmist is comparing God's Word to a lamp. How is the Bible like a lamp for us?

Say: God has given us the Bible to help us find our way—like a light in the darkness. Now let's see just how the Bible does that.

Have preteens form pairs, and give pairs a sheet of paper, a pen, and a Bible.

Say: Each pair is a team of doctors. Your patient is the person described in 2 Timothy 3:17, but that patient isn't well and not able to do "every good work." Your job is to prescribe the medicine the patient needs to survive. You'll find that medicine in 2 Timothy 3:16.

Have pairs write their recommendations.

Ask: • What's your recommended prescription?

• How can these prescriptions help us?

• How would trying to live for God without the Bible be like walking down an unfamiliar path in the dark?

The Point ➤ Say: ➤God's Word shows us how to live our everyday lives. Let's examine how it can do that for each of us.

Life Application

Let God's Word Shine on Me *(up to 10 minutes)*

Distribute papers, pens, and Bibles if needed. Have preteens reread 2 Timothy 3:16-17.

Say: We've seen several ways in this passage that God uses the Bible to help us. Write down one area in your life that you think needs more of God's light. For example, you might need more of God's light in a difficult family relationship or in your decisions about school courses.

When kids finish writing, have them fold their papers in half. Gather kids in a circle, and place the candle or flashlight in the center of the circle. Also place a Bible opened to Psalm 119:105 next to the light. Then relight the candle, or turn on the flashlight. Have students bring their folded papers and place them next to the light and Bible to symbolize receiving God's light in their lives. Encourage kids to pray silently as they bring their papers, asking God to help them find help in the Bible for their areas of need.

Wrap-Up Option 1

The Word for Life (up to 5 minutes)

Form groups of three or four. Tell groups they'll each write a slogan about how the Bible can help in their lives. Give kids paper and markers. Encourage them to think of catchy phrases such as "Warm yourself in the Sonlight of God's Word" or "The Bible: Read it, learn it, live it!"

When groups are ready, let them present their slogans. Tape the slogans to the walls, and leave them up as encouragement to live God's Word.

Distribute the "Word for the Week 2" bookmarks (see margin) to preteens, and encourage them to continue with their daily Bible readings. End your study with prayer, letting volunteers thank God for his Word.

Wrap-Up Option 2

The Word From the Word (up to 10 minutes)

Let kids share what they learned from their Bible readings this past week. Be ready to share too. Then distribute the "Word for the Week 2" bookmarks (see margin) to preteens, and encourage them to continue with their daily Bible readings. Challenge kids who haven't tried reading the Bible daily to begin this week with these Bible passages. Wrap up your session with prayer. Pray that God's Word would be especially meaningful to your students in the coming week.

Extra-Time Tips

Living in the Light—Light a candle in a holder, and set it where all the kids can see it. Turn off all the lights, and have preteens look silently at the candle for one full minute. While they look at the candle, ask them to think about how Jesus

Word for the Week 2

Monday

Matthew 10:32-39

Tuesday

John 6:35-51

Wednesday

Psalm 119:9-16

Thursday

Philippians 2:1-15

Friday

Ecclesiastes 12:1-7

Saturday

Matthew 25:31-46

gave light to the world and how God's Word still gives light to our lives. Then have students share their thoughts.

Light of the World—Have preteens wear blindfolds and perform several simple tasks, such as writing a note, pouring a glass of water, shaking hands with another person, or arranging chairs in a circle. Then have students remove their blindfolds and share how life would be different without light. Compare kids' responses to how their lives would be without the light of God's Word to guide them.

Treasure Instructions

Follow the directions below to find the hidden treasure.

Treasure Instructions

Look around the area to find a treasure.

But How Do I Find It?

The Point: ➤Learning how to use the Bible will help grow our faith.

Many preteens have a strong desire to follow God. These young adolescents have the ability to research and study increasingly difficult topics in school, but they may feel lost when trying to study the Bible on a regular basis. Use this study to introduce some basic Bible study tools preteens can use to reveal the powerful messages God has for them in his Word.

Scripture Source

2 Timothy 2:15

Paul encourages Timothy to be responsible with God's Word and to correctly handle its truths.

2 Peter 3:15-18

Peter teaches the early Christians to trust in the wisdom from God's Word and not to be misled by others who have distorted some of the passages that are hard to understand. Peter encourages Christians to grow in the grace and knowledge of Jesus.

The Study at a Glance

Section	Minutes	What Students Will Do	Supplies
Warm-Up Option 1	up to 5	**Random Reading**—Randomly pick verses to answer specific questions.	Bibles, index cards, pens
Warm-Up Option 2	up to 10	**Tough Questions**—Find answers to a quiz using various reference tools.	"Trivia Quiz" handouts (p. 31), dictionary, yesterday's newspaper, pens, Bible
Bible Connection	up to 15	**Bible Study 101**—Learn how to use a study Bible.	Study Bibles
	up to 20	**Bible Study 102**—Use Bible study tools to explore two Bible passages.	Bibles, Bible concordance, Bible dictionary or encyclopedia, Bible commentary, pens, "Bible Study Tools" handouts (p. 32), "Bible Study Scriptures" handouts (p. 33)
Life Application	up to 10	**Finding God's Answers**—Find biblical answers to specific questions preteens ask.	Bibles, Bible study tools, index cards, pens
Wrap-Up Option 1	up to 5	**Mystery Prayer**—Find and read the Lord's Prayer.	Bibles, Bible study tools
Wrap-Up Option 2	up to 10	**Bible Tool Chart**—Create a chart, outlining how they can use specific Bible study tools.	Index cards, pens or thin-tipped markers, tape, "Bible Study Tools" handouts (used in "Bible Study 102")

Before the Study

Set out study Bibles, a dictionary, pens, thin-tipped markers, index cards, tape, yesterday's newspaper, and Bible concordances, dictionaries, encyclopedias, and commentaries.

Make one photocopy of the "Bible Study Tools" handout (p. 32) and "Bible Study Scriptures" handout (p. 33) for each student.

If you choose to do Warm-Up Option 2, you'll also need a photocopy of the "Trivia Quiz" handout (p. 31) for every three or four students.

The Study

Warm-Up Option 1

Random Reading *(up to 5 minutes)*

Give preteens each an index card and a pen, and have them write down a question they'd like the Bible to answer. Let students know they'll be reading their questions to the class.

When everyone has finished, distribute Bibles.

Say: Now let's find biblical answers to our questions. Close your eyes, open your Bible, and point to a spot on the page.

Have kids read their questions and then read the verses they point to.

Ask: • How well did the verse answer your question?

• Does this seem like a good way to find answers in the Bible? Why or why not?

Say: There are much better ways to find answers in the Bible. In fact, there are a variety of tools that can help us study and understand the Bible

The Point ➤ **better. ➤Learning how to use the Bible will help grow our faith. Let's explore how to do this.**

Collect the students' questions to use in the "Finding God's Answers" activity.

Warm-Up Option 2

Tough Questions *(up to 10 minutes)*

FYI

Whenever groups discuss a list of questions, write the questions on newsprint, and tape the newsprint to the wall so groups can discuss the questions at their own pace.

Form groups of three or four. Give each group a "Trivia Quiz" handout (p. 31). Tell kids they have three minutes to find all the answers. Allow them to use a dictionary, yesterday's newspaper, and any other reference tools you've brought.

After three minutes, give the answers from the "Answers to Trivia Quiz" box in the margin on page 27. Have groups report how many questions they answered correctly.

Ask: • Was it hard finding the answers to our trivia quiz? Why or why not?

• What tools did you use to help you find the answers?

• How much harder do you think it would be without these tools?

Say: You used several resources to help you discover the answers to our trivia quiz.

Hold up a Bible.

Say: The Bible may seem to be an intimidating book because of its size and complexity. But just as we used various resources to answer the trivia quiz, there are a variety of tools that can help us study and understand the Bible better. And ➤learning how to use the Bible will help grow our faith. Let's explore how to do this.

◄ *The Point*

Bible Connection

Bible Study 101 *(up to 15 minutes)*

Form groups of five. Distribute study Bibles (at least one for each group if possible).

Say: The simplest and most basic Bible study tool is called a study Bible. In our next activity, we're going to look at different tools that can help you study the Bible in greater depth. A study Bible is easy to use because it includes a lot of additional information as you read the Bible. Let's take a look.

Instruct groups to find the beginning of a Bible book, and have students take turns reading in their groups some of the introduction material.

Ask: • What did you learn about the Bible book your group selected?

Say: The introduction of Bible books in study Bibles gives you facts such as who wrote the book, when it was written, who the book was written to, and a brief summary of the book.

Ask: • How could this information be helpful to you?

Have groups find a passage that contains notes in the margin. Examples could include Jesus' teaching about forgiveness in Matthew 18:21-22 or Jesus' asking Peter if he loves him in John 21:15-17. After groups have read the passage, have them read the margin notes about the passage they read.

Ask: • How did the margin notes help you understand the passage better?

Say: Study Bibles are a beginning tool to help understand the Bible better. But sometimes we need additional Bible study tools because the information you need may not be included in a study Bible. Let's find out more about these tools.

Bible Study 102 *(up to 20 minutes)*

Form three groups (if you have three Bible study tools), and give a Bible concordance to one group, a Bible dictionary or encyclopedia to the second group, and a Bible commentary to the third group.

ANSWERS TO TRIVIA QUIZ

1. *(Check yesterday's newspaper.)*
2. *1799*
3. *Walter Mondale*
4. *5280*
5. *(Check local TV listings.)*
6. *a fictitious name*
7. *Asia*
8. *Tennessee Valley Authority*
9. *abacus*
10. *$\frac{1}{12}$*

FYI

The hints are based on the New International Version of the Bible. If you use a different version, adjust your hints to fit your version before making photocopies of the "Bible Study Scriptures" handout (p. 33).

Give each student a photocopy of the "Bible Study Tools" handout (p. 32).

Say: To help us begin using these Bible study tools, this handout explains what some of them are and how they are used.

Have volunteers in each group read the information on the handout aloud to their groups. Offer to explain anything on the handout if necessary.

Say: I'm going to let you find the passages we'll study today. I'll give you hints and let you use the tools we have here to find the passages.

Distribute photocopies of the "Bible Study Scriptures" handout (p. 33) to each student.

Here are the Scriptures that students will be trying to find according to the hints listed on their "Bible Study Scriptures" handouts:

Passage 1 Hints

- contains the word *worker* or *workman*
- contains the word *true* or *truth*
- is in the New Testament
- is in one of the books Paul wrote
- is in 2 Timothy
- begins, "Do your best to present yourself to God as one approved…"

Passage 1: 2 Timothy 2:15

Passage 2 Hints

- contains the word *Scriptures*
- contains the word *Paul*
- is in the New Testament
- is in one of the books Peter wrote
- is in 2 Peter
- begins, "Bear in mind that our Lord's patience means salvation…"

Passage 2: 2 Peter 3:15-18

Say: In your group, find both passages and discuss what they mean. Then use the tools in your group to find out more about each passage. Record your discoveries on your handout.

Allow groups to trade Bible study tools after about four minutes. Repeat after another four minutes. Then have groups report what they found.

Ask: • What's the main message of 2 Timothy 2:15?

• What's the main message of 2 Peter 3:15-18?

• How did the tools you used help you understand the Scriptures better?

Say: These tools can help us understand Scripture. And ➤learning how to use the Bible will help grow our faith. Now we're going to see if we can find answers to your questions.

◄ *The Point*

Life Application

Finding God's Answers *(up to 10 minutes)*

If you chose the "Random Reading" activity for your Warm-Up, use kids' questions for this activity. If you did Warm-Up Option 2, provide index cards, and ask students to write on their cards one question they'd like the Bible to answer. Then gather the questions.

Sort through the questions, and choose some that kids are most likely to find answers to, using the Bible study tools you've provided. Choose one question for every four or five preteens.

Form groups of four or five. Give each group one question to answer from the Bible. If kids have trouble finding answers, give suggestions. You may want to point out that some questions don't have easy answers, even when we have Bible study tools to help us. Tell kids they may find principles to apply to specific situations instead of exact answers. Discuss briefly how the Bible's principles can apply to today's concerns.

Let groups work a few minutes, then have them report the answers to their questions.

Ask: • What new thing did you learn from this activity?

• How do you think using these tools will help you grow as a Christian?

Say: ➤Learning how to use the Bible will help grow our faith. The things you've learned about today will help you with a lifetime of Bible discovery.

◄ *The Point*

Wrap-Up Option 1

Mystery Prayer *(up to 5 minutes)*

Say: To close our study, we're going to read a prayer together. But first you have to find that prayer. It's the prayer Jesus used when he taught his disciples how to pray. It's commonly known as the Lord's Prayer.

Give kids Bibles, and have the Bible study tools available for them to use. Give hints as needed to help kids find the Lord's Prayer (Matthew 6:9-13 or Luke 11:2-4). When kids have found the prayer, read it together as your closing.

Wrap-Up Option 2

Bible Tool Chart (up to 10 minutes)

Form groups of three. Distribute index cards and pens or thin-tipped markers. Have preteens use the information on the "Bible Study Tools" handouts to make small charts that will help them know which tools to use when they want to find something in the Bible. For example, kids can write down where to look for a name, a particular word, a particular verse, or background information. Be sure each student makes a chart.

Say: You can tape your chart in the front or back of your Bible as a quick reference guide. You can use your chart to help you explore your Bible. Let's thank God for giving us his Word and the tools to help us understand it better.

Ask for a volunteer to close the study in a brief prayer.

Extra-Time Tips

Church Library Tour—Go to your church library to look at tools kids can use for studying the Bible. Have preteens look through commentaries or other study tools that are available. Encourage kids to check out some books to use for their Bible study time.

Find-It-in-the-Bible Practice—List the following Bible topics on newsprint, but don't give the references. Have preteens use Bible study tools to find the reference for each topic.

- Daniel in the lions' den (Daniel 6:16-24)
- David and Goliath (1 Samuel 17)
- The Sermon on the Mount (Matthew 5–7)
- Jesus' resurrection (John 20:1-18)
- Noah and the flood (Genesis 6:9–9:19)
- The stoning of Stephen (Acts 7:54-60)
- Manna (Exodus 16)
- Peter walking on water (Matthew 14:28-31)

TOUGH TRIVIA!

1. What was the official high temperature the day before yesterday?

2. What year did George Washington die?

3. Who was vice president under Jimmy Carter?

4. How many feet are in a mile?

5. What TV show was on NBC at 9:00 last night?

6. What's a pseudonym?

7. Of the seven continents, which is the largest in area?

8. What does TVA stand for?

9. What's a Chinese counting device made up of beads that slide on wires?

10. What proportion of a troy pound is a troy ounce?

Bible Study Tools

Check out below how the following tools can help you study the Bible. Then keep this handout handy at home for future reference. A large variety of these tools are available on CD-ROM or online as well.

Bible Concordance

What it does—A concordance lists words from the Bible in alphabetical order, then shows where those words appear in the Bible. Some concordances contain every word in every verse of the Bible. Others, such as those in the back of many Bibles, contain only the most significant words in verses.

How you can use it—You can use a concordance for at least two purposes. First, you can find places in the Bible where a particular word is used. For example, if you want to read verses that mention *sin*, look up *sin* in your concordance, then look up the Bible verses listed there.

Concordances can also help you find passages you kind of know but aren't sure where they are. For example, if you remember a verse that says something about God loving the world but don't know where to find it, you can look up *love* in your concordance. If you remember other words from the verse, you can look them up too. Before long you'll track down your verse: John 3:16.

Bible Dictionary or Encyclopedia

What is does—A Bible dictionary or encyclopedia lists biblical topics, people, and places in alphabetical order. Bible dictionaries usually cover Bible topics, such as heaven. Bible encyclopedias cover items from the Bible and also topics related to the Bible, such as biblical archeology. For each item listed, it gives historical information and explains the topics to help you understand the Bible better.

How you can use it—You can use a Bible dictionary to help you learn about people, places, or things in the Bible. For example, suppose you want to find out who the Apostle Paul was. You can look up *Paul* in a Bible dictionary, and it'll provide information about who Paul was and what he did.

Bible Commentary

What it does—A Bible commentary follows Scripture and gives comments to help us understand passages and words in the Bible. A commentary may cover one book of the Bible, the Old or New Testament, or the whole Bible.

How you can use it—You can use Bible commentaries to help you understand parts of Scripture. For example, if you're not sure what Jesus means in John 4:10 when he talks about "living water," you could look up that verse in a commentary to help you understand.

Bible Study Scriptures

Passage 1 Hints

- contains the word *worker* or *workman*
- contains the word *true* or *truth*
- is in the New Testament
- is in one of the books Paul wrote
- is in 2 Timothy
- begins, "Do your best to present yourself to God as one approved...."

Passage 1: _____

What I discovered:

_____

_____

_____

_____

_____

_____

_____

_____

_____

Passage 2 Hints

- contains the word *Scriptures*
- contains the word *Paul*
- is in the New Testament
- is in one of the books Peter wrote
- is in 2 Peter
- begins, "Bear in mind that our Lord's patience means salvation...."

Passage 2: _____

What I discovered:

_____

_____

_____

_____

_____

_____

_____

_____

_____

Personal Bible Study

The Point: ➤Personal Bible study time is important for living as Christians.

Preteens have busy lives. With increasing pressures from school and social activities, they often find little time to read the Bible.

God gave us the Bible to guide our lives. As the lives of preteens get more complex, guidance from God's Word is crucial. This study will help preteens see the importance of regular Bible study and will provide steps to help them make regular Bible study a part of their lives.

Scripture Source

Genesis 12:1-9

Abram leaves his home in obedience to God's command. After hearing God's instructions, Abram travels toward an unknown land that God has promised to show him. Abram demonstrates the strength of his relationship with God by simply hearing and obeying God's Word.

Psalm 119

The poet who wrote this psalm went into great detail about the value of God's Word. This psalm represents the longest chapter in the Bible and is structured around an acrostic poem. The psalmist begins each stanza with one of the twenty-two letters of the Hebrew alphabet, exploring every angle of the greatness of God's Word and how following it is a blessing.

Daniel 6:1-11

Daniel was committed to praying to God three times daily. Daniel's enemies set a trap for him by having the king outlaw praying to anyone but the king. But Daniel knew spending time with God was more important than obeying the king's command.

Acts 20:22-27, 32, 36

Paul prays before he begins his final journey to Rome. He expresses that testifying to the gospel of God's grace is more important than the hardships he faces in life and that God's Word can build you up and give you an inheritance.

The Study at a Glance

Section	Minutes	What Students Will Do	Supplies
Warm-Up Option 1	up to 10	**The Voice of God**—Participate in a God-sound-alike experiment.	
Warm-Up Option 2	up to 5	**What Do You Know About God?**—Take a quiz about God.	
Bible Connection	up to 10	**Relying on God**—Explore how various Bible characters relied on God.	Bibles, "Bible Journal" handouts (p. 40), pens
	up to 15	**Time in the Word**—Practice personal Bible study by exploring verses from Psalm 119.	Bibles, "Personal Bible Study Guide" handouts (p. 41), pens
Life Application	up to 10	**Commit to the Word**—Commit to study the Bible regularly.	"Bible Journal" handouts (used in "Relying on God"), "Personal Bible Study Guide" handouts (used in "Time in the Word"), pens
Wrap-Up Option 1	up to 10	**Celebrate the Scriptures!**—Enjoy snacks while singing praise songs, celebrating God's gift of the Bible.	Party snacks, praise and worship CDs, CD player
Wrap-Up Option 2	up to 10	**Quotable Quote**—Contemplate a quote about understanding the Bible.	

Before the Study

Set out Bibles and pens.

Make one photocopy of the "Bible Journal" handout (p. 40) for each student and four photocopies of the "Personal Bible Study Guide" handout (p. 41) for each student.

If you choose to do Wrap-Up Option 1, set out party snacks, praise and worship CDs, and a CD player.

The Study

Warm-Up Option 1

The Voice of God (up to 10 minutes)

After everyone arrives,

Ask: • How do you think God sounds?

Before kids respond,

Say: We're going to do a God-sound-alike experiment.

One by one, have kids come to the front of the room and say, "Let there be light!" in their best God-like voice. Don't give them any indication of what you

*Whenever groups discuss
a list of questions, write
the questions on newsprint,
and tape the newsprint to
the wall so groups can
discuss the questions at their
own pace.*

expect God's voice to sound like.

Allow each student to present his or her God-like voice. When kids have finished, discuss the following questions.

The Point ➤

Ask: • **Which voice do you think sounded like God's voice? Why?**

• **What are some reasons why you think God sounds a certain way?**

• **Most times, God probably doesn't use an audible voice to communicate to us. How does God speak to us most often today?**

Say: One of the most important ways God speaks to us today is through the Bible. And for us to know what he is saying, we need to regularly read and study his Word. ➤**Personal Bible study time is important for living as Christians. Let's find out how we can do this.**

Warm-Up Option 2

What Do You Know About God? *(up to 5 minutes)*

Say: Let's take a quiz to find out what you know about God.

Ask preteens the following questions. Pause after each question to allow students time to give answers. Give the answer to each question before asking the next question. The answers are in parentheses after the questions. Preteens will probably have trouble answering all three questions.

Ask: • **On which day of Creation did God create birds?** (The fifth day; Genesis 1:20-23)

• **How many names are used for God in the Old Testament?** (More than fifteen)

• **When did Satan speak to God?** (When discussing Job; Job 1:6–2:6)

After the last question,

The Point ➤

Say: The answers to all these questions about God are in the Bible. And so are a lot more important things we can learn about God. ➤Personal Bible study time is important for living as Christians. Let's find out how we can do this.

Bible Connection

Relying on God *(up to 10 minutes)*

Distribute a Bible, a "Bible Journal" handout (p. 40), and a pen to each preteen. Allow students to find some personal space to work on this activity. Assign one of these Bible characters and passages to each student:

- Abram (Genesis 12:1-9)
- Daniel (Daniel 6:1-11)
- Paul (Acts 20:22-27, 32, 36)

Say: Let's say you are the main character in this Bible passage. Read the situation, and think about how knowing God can give you strength while facing this situation. Write your Bible character's name on your journal page, and record your thoughts.

Allow students a few minutes to write their entries in the first section of their journals. They will use the other section during the "Commit to the Word" activity.

Ask: • How do you think your character felt in his situation?

• What did you learn about your Bible character's reliance on God?

• What are situations in life you are facing in which you need to rely on God?

Say: These people in the Bible showed us their dedication to God and his Word. And we can stay connected with God through studying his Word.

➤**Personal Bible study is important for living as Christians. Let's take some time to do this now.**

◄ *The Point*

Time in the Word *(up to 15 minutes)*

Have preteens form pairs, and provide Bibles.

Say: There is a psalm in the Bible that talks a lot about the value of God's Word. Let's take some time to explore it.

Have pairs find Psalm 119 in their Bibles. Explain how this psalm was constructed by giving the following information.

Say: This psalm is an acrostic poem. Each section begins with a letter of the Hebrew alphabet, which consists of twenty-two letters. You and your partner will each be assigned a Hebrew letter from this psalm to explore.

Assign two Hebrew letters of Psalm 119 to each pair. Each letter has eight verses. Give each student a photocopy of the "Personal Bible Study Guide" handout (p. 41). Have pairs decide who will read the passage and who will record the responses on the handout. After pairs have completed their first assigned psalm letter, have them switch roles and explore their second psalm letter. After pairs have completed studying their two psalm passages,

Ask: • What did you learn about this psalm?

• How can these discoveries help your walk with God?

The Point ➤

Say: Congratulations! You've just completed some thoughtful Bible study. You may not need to study the Bible in this much detail in every situation, but it is helpful to know how to study the Bible when the need arises. Let's make a commitment to spending quality time in God's Word because ➤personal Bible study time is important for living as Christians.

Life Application

Commit to the Word *(up to 10 minutes)*

Distribute at least three additional "Personal Bible Study Guide" handouts (p. 41) to each student.

Say: We've spent several weeks studying about the Bible. If you haven't yet, it's time to really start studying the Bible on your own. You can use these handouts to help get started.

Have students look at their "Bible Journal" handouts.

Say: If you're willing to read several Bible verses a week and study them using your "Personal Bible Study Guide" handouts, I'd like you to sign your "Bible Journal" page. You can choose how many days a week you plan to have personal Bible study time, and you may use the suggested Scripture readings from the Gospel of John as a guide to start studying your Bible.

As kids consider their commitments,

Say: For those of you who make this commitment, please give me your phone number and e-mail address before the end of this study so that I can encourage you as you read and study the Bible.

Be sure to keep track of which kids make commitments so you can call or e-mail and encourage them in their commitment to read the Bible regularly.

Before moving on to your Wrap-Up, offer to give kids more "Personal Bible Study Guide" handouts (p. 41) if and when they need them. Suggest that kids hole-punch their handouts and keep them in a three-ring binder.

Wrap-Up Option 1

Celebrate the Scriptures! *(up to 10 minutes)*

Say: Isn't it exciting that God, the Creator of the universe, wants to communicate with us? Let's celebrate that God gave us the Bible!

Distribute party snacks, and sing songs of praise and thanks. Close your time together by singing a familiar, favorite praise song.

Wrap-Up Option 2

Quotable Quote *(up to 10 minutes)*

Read aloud this quote from Mark Twain: **"Most people are bothered by those passages in Scripture which they cannot understand; but as for me, I always noticed that the passages in Scripture which trouble me most are those which I do understand."**

You may want to read the quote again for understanding and emphasis or write it down on a whiteboard so everyone can see it.

Ask: • What is Mark Twain saying in this quote?

• What's one thing you've understood in our Bible study lessons that challenges you?

• What will you do in response to that challenge?

Close with prayer, asking God to help preteens apply to their lives what they learn in the Bible.

Extra-Time Tips

Show and Tell—Before this study, use a "Personal Bible Study Guide" handout in your own personal Bible study. Then share it with your students, showing them what you discovered and how you'll apply it to your life.

Biblical Literature—Form five groups (a group can be one person). Assign one of the Bible's five major literary sections to each group (suggested books are listed in parentheses):

- History (Genesis)
- Poetry (Psalms)
- Wisdom (Proverbs)
- Epistles or letters (James)
- Prophecy (Isaiah)

Have students choose a few passages from their assigned books to read and summarize. Use the "Personal Bible Study Guide" handout (p. 41) to guide the process. Allow kids to share their discoveries.

Bible Journal

Bible character _____

_____
_____
_____
_____
_____
_____
_____
_____
_____
_____
_____
_____
_____
_____
_____

To develop my relationship with God, I commit to read and carefully study several Bible verses during the week. I promise to follow through on this commitment the best I can for the next four weeks.

Signed: _____

BIBLE STUDY PLAN FOR THE GOSPEL OF JOHN:

❏ John 1:1-14   ❏ John 3:1-21

❏ John 1:15-28   ❏ John 3:22-36

❏ John 1:29-42   ❏ John 4:1-24

❏ John 1:43-51   ❏ John 4:25-42

❏ John 2:1-11   ❏ John 4:43-54

❏ John 2:12-25

PERSONAL BIBLE STUDY GUIDE

Use the following questions to help you study your assigned passage.
Then keep the questions to help you in your own personal Bible study.

Passage: _____

What does it say? (In a nutshell, what's the message of this passage?)

_____
_____
_____
_____
_____
_____

What does it mean? (What does this passage suggest people should do to respond?)

_____
_____
_____
_____
_____

What does it mean to me? (How does this passage apply to me?)

_____
_____
_____
_____
_____

What am I going to do about it? (What will I do in response to the message of this passage?)

_____
_____
_____
_____

Changed **4** *LiFE*

This study has helped preteens see the importance of God's Word in their daily lives. Use this activity to encourage regular Bible study.

Into the Word

Set up some personal Bible study time once a week. You could rotate meeting in the homes of your preteens, or you could meet at the church. Select a Bible book to study. Good beginning choices are the Gospel of Mark or the book of James. Set up some goals for the study time, and provide the Bible study tools that were used in the third study of this book. Follow up weekly with the kids involved in the study, and give encouraging phone or e-mail messages during the week. Have preteens involved in the study share their experiences with your class, and encourage new students to join the study time.

EVALUATION FOR
Faith 4 Life: The Bible and Me

Please help Group Publishing, Inc., continue to provide innovative and useful resources for ministry. Please take a moment to fill out this evaluation and mail or fax it to us. Thanks!

Group Publishing, Inc.
Attention: Product Development
P.O. Box 481
Loveland, CO 80539
Fax: (970) 292-4370

● ● ●

1. As a whole, this book has been (circle one)
not very helpful   *very helpful*
1   2   3   4   5   6   7   8   9   10

2. The best things about this book:

3. Ways this book could be improved:

4. Things I will change because of this book:

5. Other books I'd like to see Group publish in the future:

6. Would you be interested in field-testing future Group products and giving us your feedback? If so, please fill in the information below:

Name _____

Church Name _____

Denomination _____ Church Size _____

Church Address _____

City_____ State _____ ZIP _____

Church Phone _____

E-mail _____

Look for the Whole Family of Faith 4 Life Bible Studies!

Preteen Books

Being Responsible
Getting Along With Others
God in My Life
Going Through Tough Times

How to Make Great Choices
Peer Pressure
The Bible and Me
Why God Made Me

Junior High Books

Becoming a Christian
Fighting Temptation
Finding Your Identity
Friends

God's Purpose for Me
My Life as a Christian
Understanding the Bible
Who Is God?

Senior High Books

Applying God's Word
Believing in Jesus
Family Matters
Is There Life After High School?

Prayer
Sexuality
Sharing Your Faith
Your Christian ID

Coming Soon...

For Preteens

Building Friendships
Handling Conflict

Succeeding in School
What's a Christian?

For Junior High

Choosing Wisely
How to Pray

My Family Life
Sharing Jesus

For Senior High

Christian Character
Following Jesus

Worshipping 24/7
Your Relationships

Visit your local Christian bookstore or contact Group Publishing, Inc. at 800-447-1070. www.grouppublishing.com

More Preteen Ministry Resources!

The Preteen Worker's Encyclopedia of Bible-Teaching Ideas

Make the New Testament come alive to your preteens and help them discover Bible truths in a big way! In this comprehensive collection, you get nearly 200 creative ideas and activities including: object lessons, skits, games, devotions, service projects, creative prayers, affirmations, creative readings, retreats, parties, trips and travel, and music ideas.

Flexible for any group setting, you'll easily find the perfect idea with helpful Scripture and theme indexes.

ISBN 0-7644-2425-4

Dynamic Preteen Ministry

Gordon West & Becki West

Maximize ministry to preteens as they make the difficult transition from childhood to adolescence. Both children's and youth workers will better understand the minds and emotions of 10- to 14-year-olds, "bridge the gap" between children's ministry and youth ministry.

ISBN 0-7644-2084-4

The Ultimate Book of Preteen Devotions

Take the challenge of ministering to preteens to the edge! They're sure to connect with these 75 Bible-based devotions. From setting goals, to materialism, to dealing with divorce—these topics and many others are included in the 6 big themes found in this ultimate book:

- Faith
- School
- Friends
- My World
- Family
- Special Days

Plus, easy-prep devotional activities use different learning styles—and multiple intelligences—to reach all preteens. Scripture index included.

ISBN 0-7644-2588-9

Order today from your local Christian bookstore, online at www.grouppublishing.com or write:
Group Publishing, P.O. Box 485, Loveland, CO 80539-0485.

Connect with Preteens In Dynamic Ways!

No-Miss Lessons for Preteen Kids

Here are 22 faith-building lessons that keep 5th- and 6th-graders coming back! Children's workers get active-learning lessons dealing with faith…self-esteem…relationships…choices…and age-appropriate service projects that any preteen class can do!

ISBN 0-7644-2015-1

No-Miss Lessons for Preteen Kids 2

Enjoy ministering to your preteens like never before! This flexible resource features 20 action-packed, easy-to-teach lessons that talk about the stuff of life in the preteen world. Stuff like the Internet and media, how to get along with family and friends, faith foundations based on God and Jesus, and many others! These lessons and the 13 bonus, "can't-miss" service project ideas will challenge kids, grow their faith, and give them practical ideas for living out their deepening faith in meaningful ways!

ISBN 0-7644-2290-1

The Ultimate Book of Preteen Games

They're not children. Not teenagers. What do you do with preteens? Have a blast! Start with these 100 games they'll love! In the process, you'll break down cliques, build relationships, explore relevant Bible truths, give thought-provoking challenges, and have high-energy fun!

ISBN 0-7644-2291-X

Order today from your local Christian bookstore, online at www.grouppublishing.com or write:
Group Publishing, P.O. Box 485, Loveland, CO 80539-0485.